Prompts About Limiting Self Belief: What is getting in the way of my living the life I want?

How do I hold myself back?

What are habits keeping me from being productive?

What fear am I most struggling to overcome?

What could my future look like without this limitation? Write about an ideal day.

What do I need to let go of? (Fears, toxic energies/relationships)
What ten things am I grateful for today?

What 5 things do I excel at?

What are 6 ways I can go out of my comfort zone this year?

How would I describe myself to someone who hasn't met me before?

Without this limitation, where could I be in 5 years?

Without this limitation, where could I be in 10 years?

What is something I've always wanted to try but haven't because of fear? Why am I afraid?

What is draining my energy?

What do I want to learn more about?

What is a short term goal I am confident I could achieve?

What was my biggest fear when I was younger? Has it changed?

What makes me the most angry, or frustrated and why?

What was my most productive month or week recently?

Who inspires me and why?

What is one reality I need to come to peace with?

Write down something I am stressed about.

What was my most vivid dream recently?

What are three things you don't do often, but would like to do?

What was the last thing you celebrated?

What is my biggest regret?

What three words describe me best?

What do I admire about myself?

What am I doing when I am at my happiest?

What has stopped me in my tracks from progress before?

What have I learned from this journaling experience?

Prompts About Self Confidence: What does confidence mean to you?

What are five things you love about yourself?

What is a compliment that you receive often? Do you agree or disagree and why?

Who is/are your greatest role model(s)?

Do you see some of their qualities in yourself?

Name a friend you are especially grateful to have in your life. What are their qualities that make them such a great friend?

Reflect on something you need more of in your life.

Why does this come to mind?

What does your ideal day look like?

What are 3 passions/skills that you excel at?

What unhealthy habits do you need to release?

Reflect on a relationship/friendship that may have been or may be toxic.

Why is it important to release toxic relationships/friendships?

Reflect on fears that may have been or may be holding you back. Why is it important to work through and release these fears?

What is your biggest struggle with loving yourself?

What do you need to forgive yourself for?

What things make you feel happy to be alive?

Where in life do you need to slow down and take your time?

What would your younger self be proud of you for today?

What is something you need to get rid of?

What is something you need to start saying "yes" to?

How are you making the world a better place in your day to day life?

How can you give yourself a break today? (Mentally, emotionally, physically).

Take a selfie, just as you are. Find one thing to love about it.

Name a thing you love about your body.

A thing you love about your personality.

What does your support system look like?

How can you make it stronger?

What is the most loving thing you've ever done for yourself?

What is something you wish someone would say to you?

What's something you're working on believing that you deserve?

How can you start setting boundaries in your life?

What things make you feel bad but you find yourself doing anyways?

What beliefs do you want to live your life by?

Going forward how can you commit to loving yourself?

What have you learned from this journaling experience?

Prompts About Gratitude: What does gratitude mean?

How can/do you show gratitude?

Name a highlight of your day.

What was one thing that made you smile today?

What are you most grateful for and why?

What is one thing you love about your significant other?

What is one thing you love about your parents?

What is one thing you love about your friends?

What is your favorite childhood memory?

Name a favorite song. Why is it your favorite?

Name a favorite movie.

Why does this movie come to mind?

Recall a time you needed encouragement and received it.

What is one skill you are grateful for?

What is your favorite season? Why is it your favorite?

How has technology made your life easier?

Name someone who was kind to you today.

Name something that made you laugh today.

Name someone or something who inspires you.

Reflect on something or someone that/who helps you stay healthy.

Name a great thing that happened this week.

Reflect on something or someone you may take for granted.

Name something new you learned recently.

What is something you enjoy about your work, or appreciate about a coworker?

Name something that lifts your spirits on a rough day.

What is your favorite thing on your mind when you wake up in the morning?

What is an activity you especially enjoy? Why do you enjoy it so much?

When you find yourself out in nature, what do you enjoy most about the experience?

What is something you have been putting off and finally did/accomplished recently?

Name a book you are grateful for reading?

Name a favorite place you like to visit.

What is one thing you learned from this journaling experience?

www.ingramcontent.com/pod-product-compliance
Lightning Source LLC
LaVergne TN
LVHW012113070526
838202LV00056B/5717
* 9 7 8 3 7 4 9 7 5 5 3 5 6 *